P9-DCT-259

My First Book of
QUESTIONS
and
ANSWERS

by Colin Clark
Illustrations by Tony Gibbons

Brown Watson
ENGLAND

WHICH IS THE LARGEST ANIMAL?

The largest animal in the world today is the Blue Whale, which is actually the largest animal that has *ever* lived. In 1947, a Russian whaling ship caught a Blue Whale that weighed over 190 tonnes. An even bigger Blue Whale had been caught back in 1909. To save these magnificent creatures from being wiped out, people are no longer supposed to hunt them.

WHO WAS THE OUTLAW OF SHERWOOD FOREST?

The legendary outlaw was none other than Robin Hood, who fought for the poor against the rich, evil lords who oppressed the weak, whilst King Richard the Lionheart was away from England on a Crusade. When Robin was declared an outlaw, he hid in the depths of Sherwood Forest, and gathered around him a band of 'Merrie Men', including Little John, Will Scarlett, and fat Friar Tuck. Robin's true love was Maid Marian.

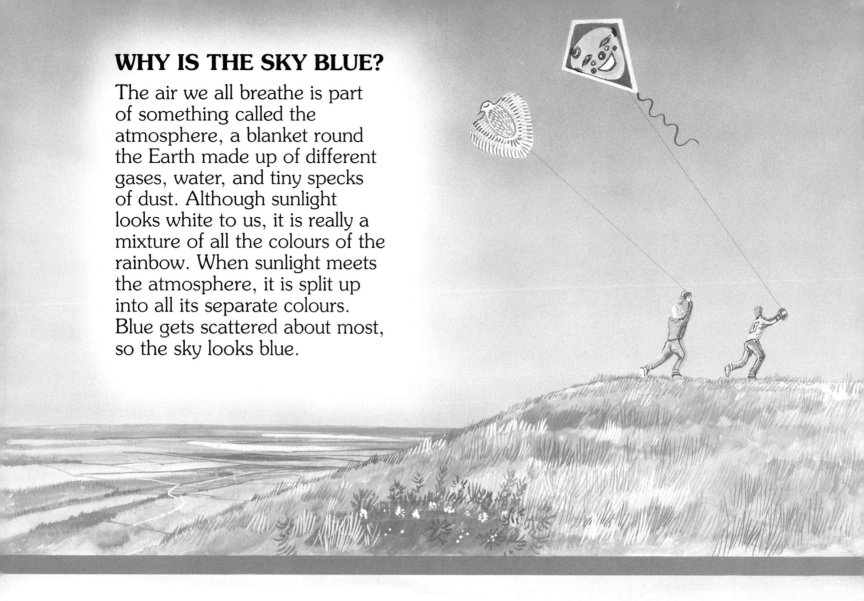

WHY IS THE SKY BLUE?

The air we all breathe is part of something called the atmosphere, a blanket round the Earth made up of different gases, water, and tiny specks of dust. Although sunlight looks white to us, it is really a mixture of all the colours of the rainbow. When sunlight meets the atmosphere, it is split up into all its separate colours. Blue gets scattered about most, so the sky looks blue.

WHERE DOES SAND COME FROM?

The Earth on which we all live has existed for millions of years. During all that time, big rocks have been under attack; from strong winds, falling rain, frost, and the constant beating of the waves. These attacks have broken off countless, little pieces of rock, which have been rubbed up against each other for so long that they are now tiny grains of sand.

3

WHO LIVES IN BUCKINGHAM PALACE?

A palace is a very large, splendid house. Very important, or very rich, people live in palaces. Buckingham Palace is in the centre of London. It has 600 rooms, and has been the home of the kings and queens of Britain since 1837. Queen Elizabeth and her husband, Prince Philip, live there now. Whenever they are at home, you will see a flag, called the Royal Standard, flying over the palace, and red-coated soldiers standing outside as sentries, and marching up and down. They are the Queen's Guard. People from all over the world make their way to Buckingham Palace to see the Guards and take pictures of them. On special occasions, they also wait to see the Queen in the magnificent, horse-drawn royal coach.

WHO LIVES IN THE WHITE HOUSE?

The White House is in Washington, the country's capital, and it is the official home of the President of the United States of America. The president lives there today. Its site was chosen by the first President, George Washington, and it is the oldest public building in the city. Its cornerstone was laid in 1792, and it was completed in 1801. It is built of stone and painted white, which is where its name comes from. During the war between Britain and the United States in 1814, British troops burned the White House, and it had to be restored later. In 1948-52, part of it had to be rebuilt, when it was discovered that it was in danger of collapse. It is surrounded by 7 hectares of carefully laid out lawns, gardens, trees and fountains.

WHEN IS HALLOWE'EN?

November 1st is All Saints' Day, a famous and historic Christian feast day. Another name for All Saints' Day is All Hallows' Day, as 'hallow' is an old word for saint. The evening before, the evening of October 31st, is All Hallows' Eve, or Hallowe'en. The custom of dressing up as witches or ghosts on that evening dates back to much older times, before Christianity.

WHAT WAS A DINOSAUR?

Dinosaur is a Greek word, meaning 'terrible lizard'. Dinosaurs were the reptiles who ruled the Earth for over 150 million years, from 230 to 65 million years ago. Some were peaceful plant-eaters, others were terrifying flesh-eaters. They varied in length, from less than a metre to almost 30 metres, and they lived all over the world. Brontosaurus, Tyrannosaurus, and Iguanodon are the names of dinosaurs.

WHAT IS A SHADOW?

The only reason that we can see anything at all is because there is light. In total darkness, we would see nothing. All light travels in straight lines, called rays. Light does not bend round corners. So, if there is a lamp in a room, and we stand between the lamp and the wall, we will see our shadow on the wall. We are stopping the light from reaching the dark part of the wall. The light cannot bend around us.

WHAT IS AN ICEBERG?

Look at a globe of the Earth, and you will see the North Pole at the top, and the South Pole at the bottom. Both places are freezing cold, with ice all around. Sometimes a great piece of ice breaks off and floats away to sea. This is an iceberg. Icebergs can take years to melt, and are very dangerous to ships. One enormous iceberg was as big as all of Belgium!

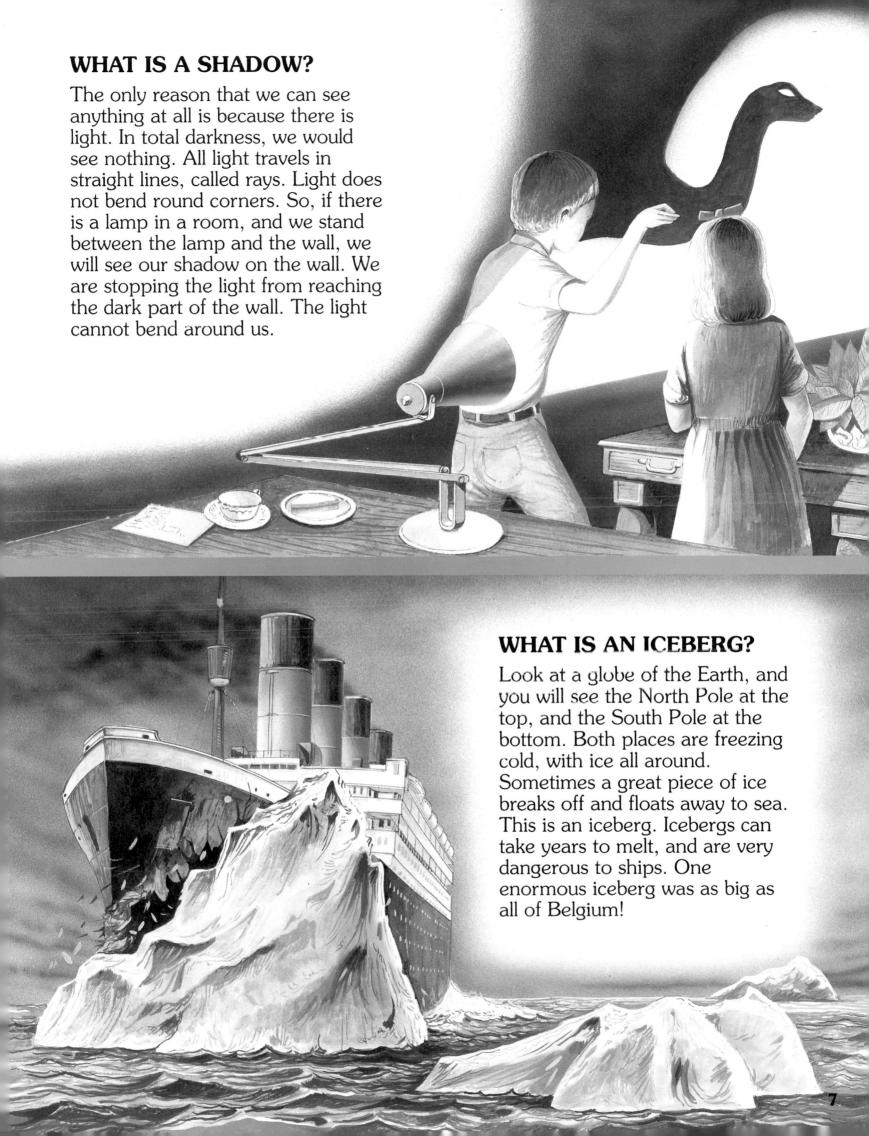

WHAT IS A VOLCANO?

Beneath our feet lie soil and sand, then the rock-solid crust of the earth. This crust is like the skin of a balloon, only it's not holding in air, but miles and miles of melted rock, and boiling gas. Sometimes this molten rock forces its way up to the surface, and bursts out of a hole in the crust, called a volcano. Volcanoes often cause much death and destruction.

WHICH IS THE TALLEST ANIMAL?

The tallest animals alive today are giraffes. Some are over 6 metres high. Giraffes are found in the wild on the grassy plains of Africa, where their long necks enable them to eat leaves and twigs from the tall acacia trees. This long neck has only 7 bones in it, so it does not bend very much. To lower its head for a drink, a giraffe has to spread its front legs wide apart.

WHAT IS CORAL?

If you ever go swimming underwater in warm, tropical seas, you will see coral. For hundreds of years, scientists thought that coral was a plant, which grew and grew until it had formed a reef, or ridge, in the sea. Then it was discovered that each tiny piece of coral is actually the chalky skeleton of a little animal, called a polyp. When the polyp dies, the skeleton remains. Countless millions of coral skeletons make a coral reef.

WHO WAS AESOP?

Aesop's Fables are short, simple animal stories which have a moral, or message, about human behaviour. They date back to Ancient Greece, 600 hundred years before Christ. It is thought that Aesop was a very observant slave, with a keen eye for human failings. The Boy Who Cried 'Wolf', The Hare and The Tortoise, and The Fox and The Grapes are just some of Aesop's Fables.

9

CAN ALL BIRDS FLY?

No! The largest bird alive today, the Ostrich, cannot fly. Nor can Kiwis, Rheas, Cassowaries, nor Emus. These species have no keel in their breastbone: that is, no broad, strong bone to which are attached the muscles needed to power the wings. Penguins do have this keel, and, 150 million years ago, their ancestors could fly. But the penguins' keel now supports the flipper muscles, for swimming, not for flying.

HOW DO WE BREATHE?

Breathing takes place through the lungs. We have two lungs in our chest. We suck in air through the nose and mouth, down the windpipe, into the lungs. The lungs expand, and the air passes into smaller and smaller tubes in them, until it reaches tiny spaces where our blood takes from it the oxygen that keeps our bodies working. Then we breathe out the waste gas, carbon dioxide, that our body does not want.

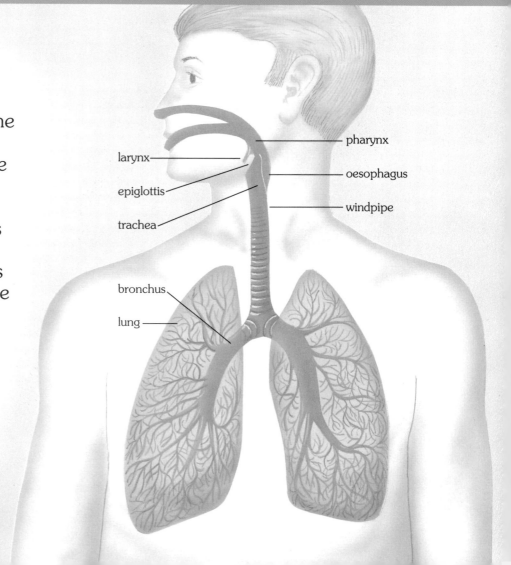

larynx
epiglottis
trachea
pharynx
oesophagus
windpipe
bronchus
lung

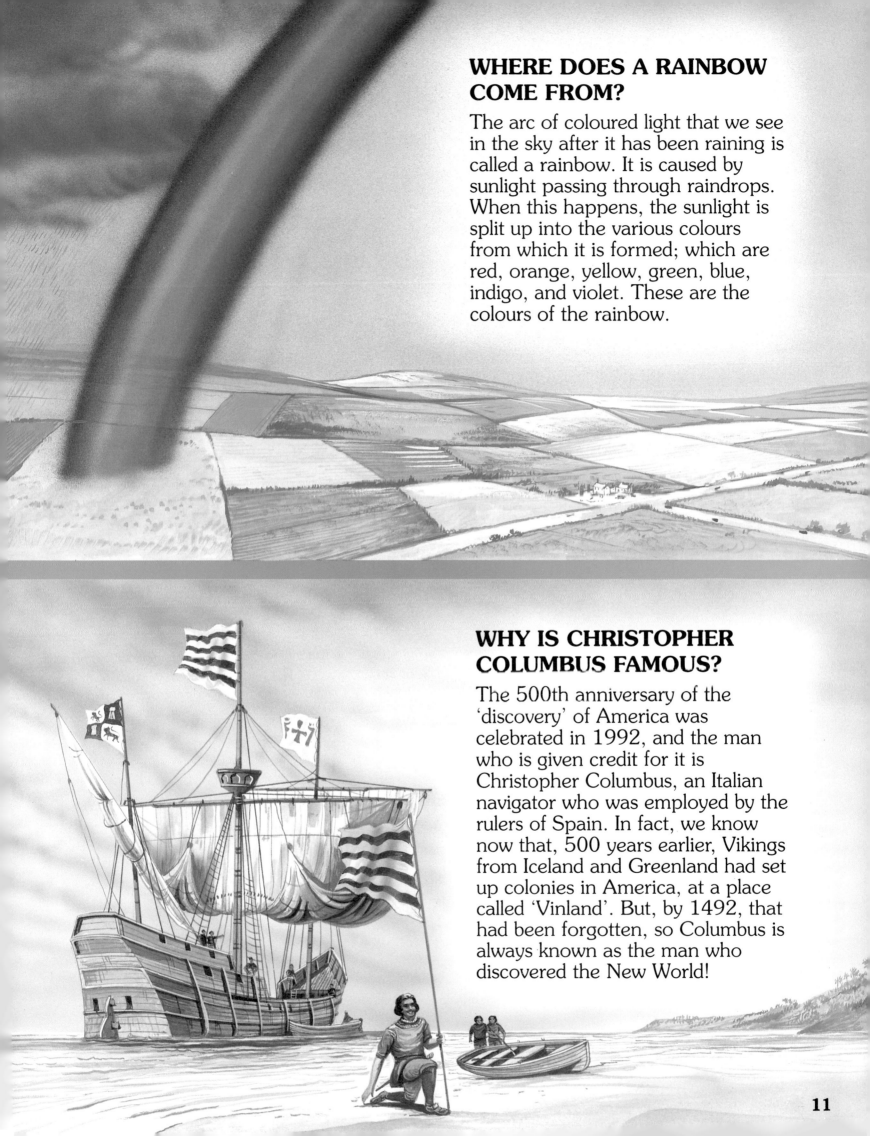

WHERE DOES A RAINBOW COME FROM?

The arc of coloured light that we see in the sky after it has been raining is called a rainbow. It is caused by sunlight passing through raindrops. When this happens, the sunlight is split up into the various colours from which it is formed; which are red, orange, yellow, green, blue, indigo, and violet. These are the colours of the rainbow.

WHY IS CHRISTOPHER COLUMBUS FAMOUS?

The 500th anniversary of the 'discovery' of America was celebrated in 1992, and the man who is given credit for it is Christopher Columbus, an Italian navigator who was employed by the rulers of Spain. In fact, we know now that, 500 years earlier, Vikings from Iceland and Greenland had set up colonies in America, at a place called 'Vinland'. But, by 1492, that had been forgotten, so Columbus is always known as the man who discovered the New World!

Earth rotating

Earth rotating   Sunrise

At sunrise,
the rotation of the earth
causes us to see the sun
'rising' over the horizon

At midday,
the sun shines
directly overhead

WHY DOES THE SUN RISE AND SET?

The Earth on which we live is going round and round all the time in space. If we can imagine a straight line, called an axis, through the middle of the ball that is the Earth, then we say that the Earth is rotating round its axis.

The Earth is also moving around the Sun, which gives us light. As the part of the Earth we live on rotates towards the Sun, we see the Sun 'rising' in the sky. Then we have plenty of light as our part of the Earth is facing the Sun. It is our daytime.

Midday

Sun

Earth rotating   Sunset

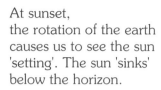

At sunset,
the rotation of the earth
causes us to see the sun
'setting'. The sun 'sinks'
below the horizon.

But the Earth keeps on rotating round its axis. As it rolls on round, it takes us away again from the Sun. Then we think we see the Sun 'setting', and it becomes dark. For us, it is night. Of course, in another part of the world, they are getting the Sun's light then. For people who live there, it is their daytime.

It takes 24 hours for the Earth to rotate once round its axis. From sunrise or sunset on one day, 24 hours will go by before it is sunrise or sunset on the next. A day will have passed.

WHERE DOES RAIN COME FROM?

When you boil a kettle, you will see steam coming out of the spout. The heat has turned some of the water into vapour. In the same way, the heat from the Sun turns some of the water in seas and lakes and rivers into vapour. The vapour gathers together to form clouds. When the clouds cool, the vapour in them turns back into water, and then falls as rain.

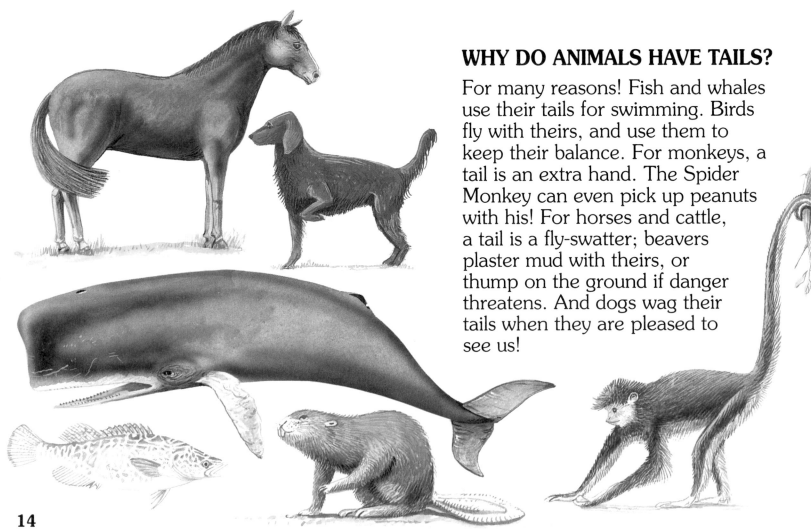

WHY DO ANIMALS HAVE TAILS?

For many reasons! Fish and whales use their tails for swimming. Birds fly with theirs, and use them to keep their balance. For monkeys, a tail is an extra hand. The Spider Monkey can even pick up peanuts with his! For horses and cattle, a tail is a fly-swatter; beavers plaster mud with theirs, or thump on the ground if danger threatens. And dogs wag their tails when they are pleased to see us!

WHO LIVES IN IGLOOS?

An igloo is a circular hut made out of blocks of snow. It is dome-shaped, has a narrow tunnel for an entrance, and a block of ice for a window. There is a small hole in the roof to let out the smoke from a fire. Igloos are very warm shelters, and they are used by the native inhabitants of the frozen north, the Eskimos, who live in Siberia, Alaska, Canada and Greenland.

WHY DO WE SNEEZE?

We cannot sneeze at will. Sneezing just happens; when we breathe in some dust, or when we have a cold or infection. The sensitive lining inside our nose gets irritated. We take a deep breath. When our lungs are full of air, our windpipe closes, our stomach muscles compress the air, then our windpipe opens again, and the air flies out suddenly, in a sneeze, which blows the irritation away from the lining of our nose.

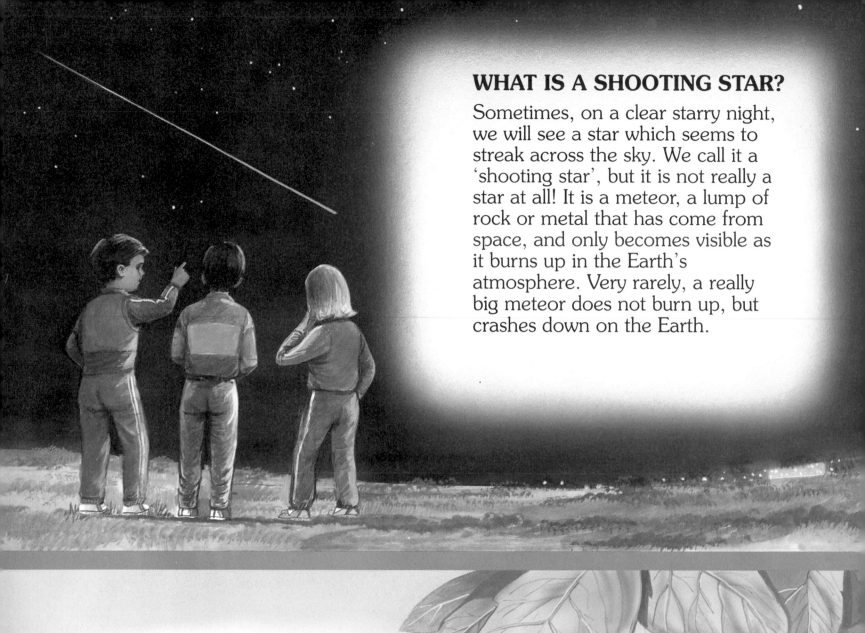

WHAT IS A SHOOTING STAR?

Sometimes, on a clear starry night, we will see a star which seems to streak across the sky. We call it a 'shooting star', but it is not really a star at all! It is a meteor, a lump of rock or metal that has come from space, and only becomes visible as it burns up in the Earth's atmosphere. Very rarely, a really big meteor does not burn up, but crashes down on the Earth.

WHY DO SPIDERS SPIN WEBS?

The spider's web is a sticky trap. Underneath the spider's body, there are tiny openings from which it can produce very fine, strong silk thread. The spider fastens the end of this thread to something firm, like a twig. Then the spider goes round and round, spinning a wheel of silk. Afterwards it fixes 'spokes' to this wheel. Then it waits until an unfortunate fly gets stuck on the sticky thread. It is the spider's lunchtime!

WHO WERE THE KNIGHTS OF THE ROUND TABLE?

A thousand years ago, stories were first told of King Arthur and his knights. He was said to have proved his right to become king of Britain by pulling the great sword Excalibur out of the stone. To protect the weak, Arthur gathered around him the finest knights in the land, and to prevent any arguments about who was most important, there was no head to the table. King Arthur and his knights sat at a round table.

WHAT IS THE STATUE OF LIBERTY?

On an island, just across from New York, there is a great statue of a woman holding high the torch of freedom: it is called the Statue of Liberty. The statue was given, in 1886, to the people of the United States of America by the people of France. The Statue of Liberty is a national monument, clearly visible from New York, and a prominent landmark for anyone approaching the city by air or sea.

WHAT ARE SNOWFLAKES?

At the temperatures below freezing, some of the water vapour which makes up the clouds will become solid, forming tiny crystals that are called snowflakes. Every single snowflake is different from every other one. No two crystals of snow are alike, but they usually occur in one of six different forms: needles, columns and groups of columns, plates, branched plates, combined plates and columns, and irregular lumps.

WHO ARE THE PYGMIES?

In Central Africa, there are a number of tribes with heights averaging no more than 1.5 metres. They are called Pygmies, from the Ancient Greek word 'pygmaios', which was a measure of distance between the elbow and the knuckles. There are less than 30,000 pygmies left alive today, and they are in danger of becoming extinct. At one time in the past, pygmies were probably the only inhabitants of the Congo river valley.

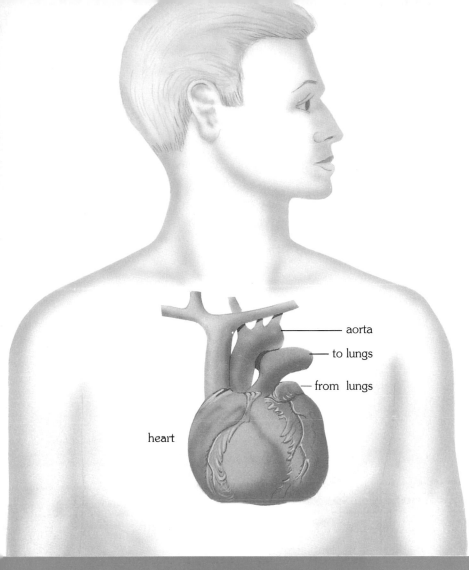

WHAT DOES OUR HEART DO?

Our heart is a big pump. We have a heart in order to move blood round our body. It is really just a very strong group of muscles, which squeeze the blood inside the heart, and force it out to every part of the body. After the blood has reached all the different parts of the body, it returns to the heart again, where, refilled with the oxygen from the lungs that the body needs, it is pumped out again. This process is called the circulation of the blood.

aorta

to lungs

from lungs

heart

CAN FISH HEAR SOUNDS?

When we hear a sound, we are really picking up vibrations in the air, called waves. Sound does not travel through a vacuum. It needs something, like air, to enable it to move from one place to another. Water will also allow sound to travel through it. Fish can hear these sounds in water through their ears, and they can also detect changes in the sound waves, through a series of holes called a lateral line, down each side of their bodies.

WHAT IS THE VATICAN?

The Vatican is an independent state inside Italy which has an area of just 44 hectares. Mainly, it consists of the great church of St Peter's, the magnificent square in front of it, and the Vatican Palace and Museum. The Vatican exists as a separate state because the Pope lives there. The Pope is the head of the largest Christian Church, the Roman Catholic Church, and the Catholic Church is run from the Vatican. The Vatican is full of great works of art; famous statues, like the *Pieta* by Leonardo da Vinci, showing the body of Christ in the arms of his mother, and paintings, like those by Michelangelo on the walls and ceiling of the Sistine Chapel, showing the Creation of the World, and the Last Judgment. The Vatican even has its own army, the Pope's bodyguards, called the Swiss Guard.

WHAT IS THE UNITED NATIONS?

The United Nations is a world organisation, and its members are all those countries who think that it is better to talk about disagreements than to fight over them. It began in 1945 with 50 members. Now there are around 180 members, meeting in the General Assembly at the headquarters in New York. The United Nations Organisation, or UNO, does not collect taxes, but relies, for the money it needs to do its work, on contributions from its members. It has no army of its own. It calls upon troops from its member countries, when it has peacekeeping work to do. Within UNO, there are different departments, called agencies, which deal with important matters like world health, education and the arts, and helping poor countries to grow enough food for their people to eat.

WHO WAS THE FIRST MAN TO FLY?

Orville and Wilbur Wright were brothers, who lived in the United States less than 100 years ago. They wanted to prove that man could fly in an engine-powered machine. They took time off from their cycle business, and built a simple aircraft called Flyer. At Kitty Hawk in North Carolina, on December 17th, 1903, Orville Wright made the first controlled flight in history. It lasted for about 12 seconds!

WHAT IS AN EARTHQUAKE?

An earthquake is a shaking of the Earth's crust, usually where there is a crack, or fault, in it. Volcanoes, which burst out through openings in the crust, also cause earthquakes. Many earthquakes occur underwater. Scientific instruments can detect about 500,000 shocks each year, but we could only feel about 100,000. Luckily, less than a thousand cause any damage. In 1976, over 700,000 people were killed in the Tangshan earthquake in China.

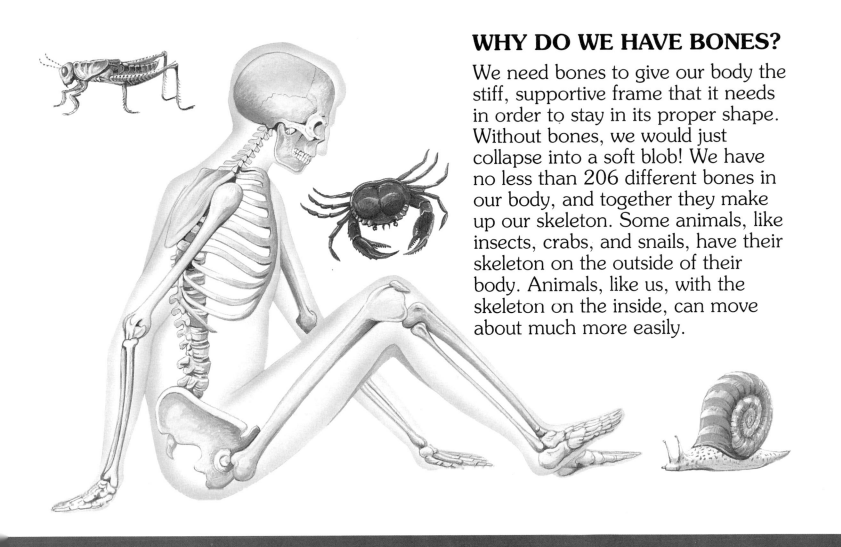

WHY DO WE HAVE BONES?

We need bones to give our body the stiff, supportive frame that it needs in order to stay in its proper shape. Without bones, we would just collapse into a soft blob! We have no less than 206 different bones in our body, and together they make up our skeleton. Some animals, like insects, crabs, and snails, have their skeleton on the outside of their body. Animals, like us, with the skeleton on the inside, can move about much more easily.

WHAT IS A MAMMAL?

Of all the creatures on Earth, the most advanced is Man. Man is a mammal; and so are cats and dogs, dolphins and elephants, giraffes and goats, hamsters, hedgehogs, weasels and whales. There are over 4,000 species of mammals. All mammals have warm blood, breathe air, and the mothers give milk to their young. Most mammals have hair, and their young are born alive. The primates, like apes, gorillas, monkeys, and Man, are the most intelligent mammals.

WHAT IS KEPT IN FORT KNOX?

Throughout history, people have tried to get their hands on gold, as a way of becoming rich. Countries do the same now. The most powerful country in the world is the United States of America, and America has the world's largest store of gold. It is kept, carefully guarded, at Fort Knox, in the state of Kentucky. The storerooms there were specially built, and reinforced with steel and concrete to keep out robbers.

WHAT ARE THE CROWN JEWELS?

The Crown Jewels consist of all the priceless objects, like crowns and sceptres, called regalia, and the jewellery, belonging to the British kings and queens. The Crown Jewels are on display in the Tower of London, and include some of the world's finest diamonds, such as the Cullinan diamond, and the Star of Africa. The Imperial State Crown alone contains over 3,000 diamonds and pearls, as well as other precious stones.

WHERE IS THE FASTEST TRAIN?

The fastest train running on normal railway lines is the French TGV (*Train à Grande Vitesse*). In a trial run, it has travelled at 380 kilometres per hour, and, with passengers aboard, it has reached speeds of 270 km/h. In Japan, there is an experimental train which does not run on rails at all. It is kept up off its track by magnetic levitation. Only when it is not moving, or is starting or stopping, does it touch the track. It has travelled at over 400 km/h.

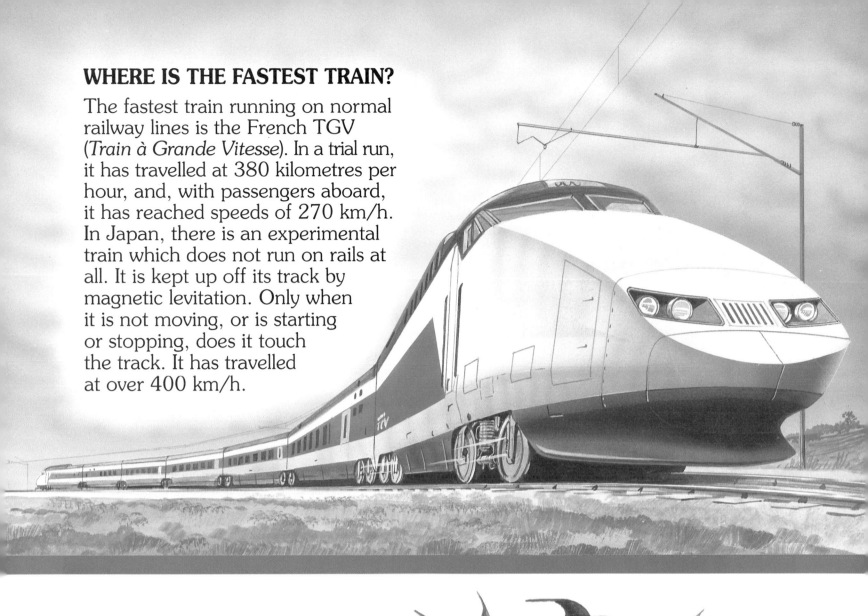

WHICH IS THE FASTEST ANIMAL?

The fastest moving of all animals is the Peregrine Falcon. This hunting bird dives on its prey from a great height. One falcon was measured with scientific instruments as diving at a speed of over 350 kilometres per hour. Some Swifts can actually fly at about 170 km/h. The fastest animal on land is the Cheetah, which can cover short distances at over 100 km/h. Fastest in water is a species of tuna, which can swim at 70 km/h . . . for a few seconds!

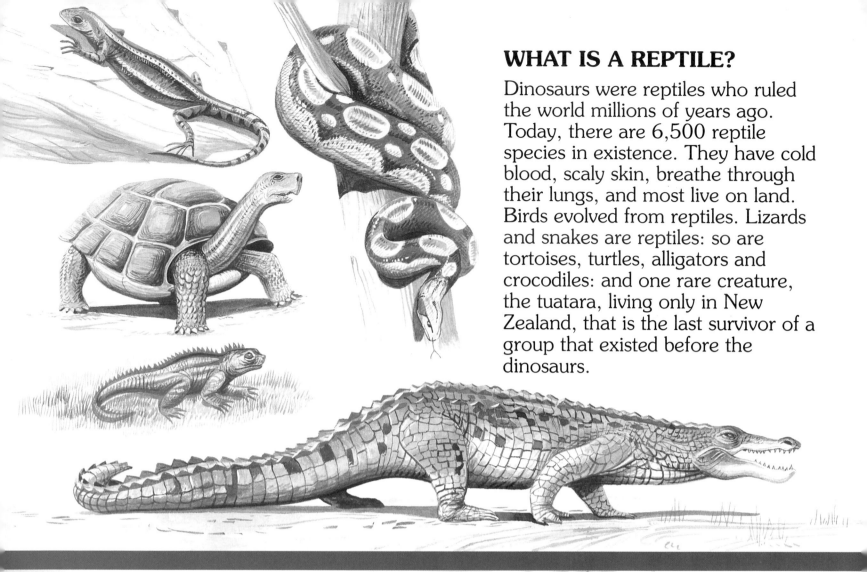

WHAT IS A REPTILE?

Dinosaurs were reptiles who ruled the world millions of years ago. Today, there are 6,500 reptile species in existence. They have cold blood, scaly skin, breathe through their lungs, and most live on land. Birds evolved from reptiles. Lizards and snakes are reptiles: so are tortoises, turtles, alligators and crocodiles: and one rare creature, the tuatara, living only in New Zealand, that is the last survivor of a group that *existed* before the dinosaurs.

WHAT ARE SOUND WAVES?

Sound is a vibration in the air around us which our ears detect. If a violin string is plucked, each quiver of the string causes a series of movements, called waves, in the air: just like waves rippling out from the splash made by a stone in a pond. The number of times the string moves or vibrates each second is called the frequency, or wavelength, of the sound. When these waves reach a part of our ear called the diaphragm, that starts to vibrate at the same frequency, which enables us to hear the sound.

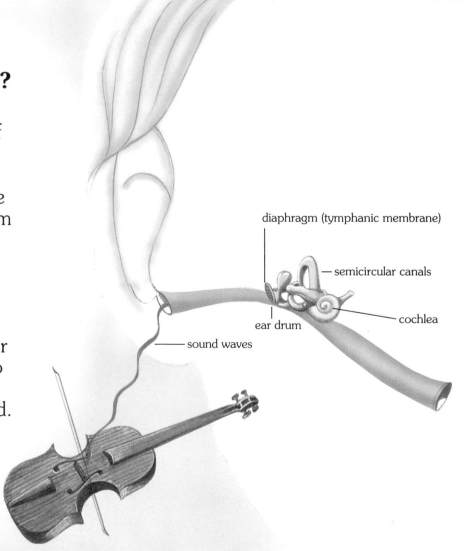

diaphragm (tymphanic membrane)

semicircular canals

cochlea

ear drum

sound waves

HOW MANY PEOPLE ARE THERE?

We can only make a guess at the total number of people in the world at any one time, because that number is estimated to be increasing by over 150 per minute! In 1987, the United Nations decided that a baby in Yugoslavia had become the world's 5 billionth inhabitant. By 1990, it is thought that there were 5¼ billion people on Earth. By the year 2,000, the total could be over 6 billion, or about 6,500,000,000! China has the most; over 1 billion in 1987, increasing by 35,000 per day!

WHAT IS OIL?

Crude oil is a liquid found in the Earth's crust. As it comes out of the ground, it is brown or black, and thick. From it we get petrol, and all our fuel and heating oils. Millions of years ago in the Earth's history, countless tiny sea animals and plants lived and died. Their remains were covered by layers of mud, until they were under so much pressure that they went through a chemical change. They turned into oil, which soaked through the underground rocks and gathered in vast pools; becoming our oilfields.

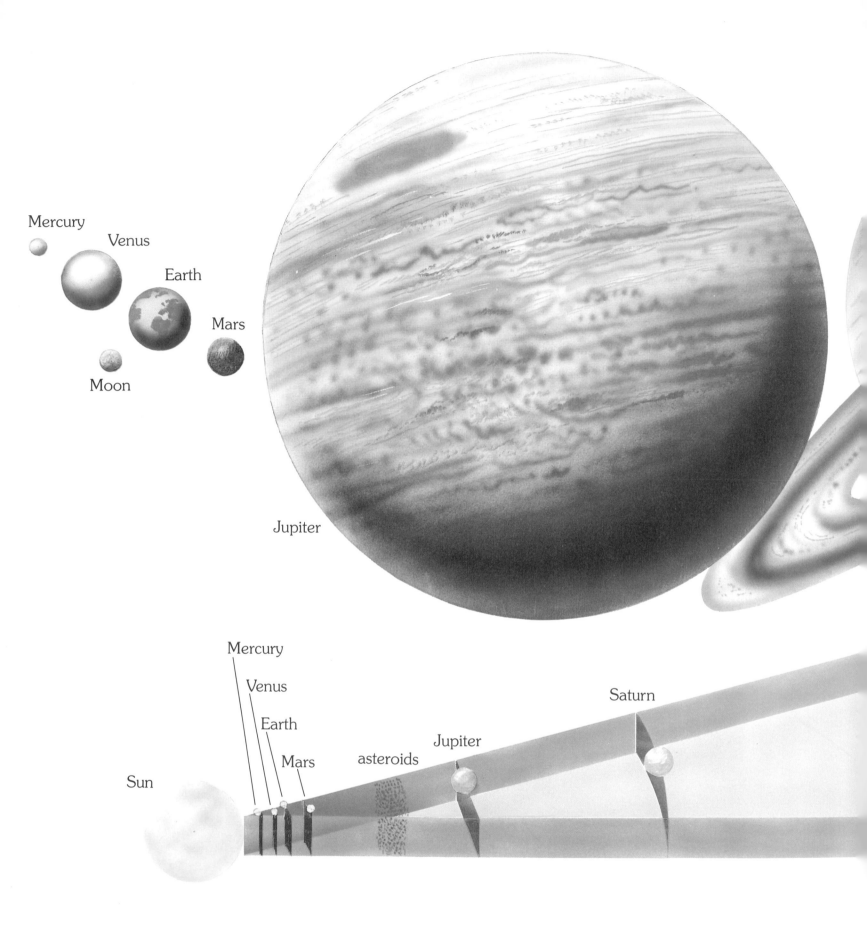

Mercury

Venus

Earth

Moon

Mars

Jupiter

Mercury

Venus

Earth

Mars

asteroids

Jupiter

Saturn

Sun

WHAT IS THE SOLAR SYSTEM?

Our Earth is a planet; which is a body in space going round a larger body, the Sun. The Sun has a family of nine planets revolving around it, plus some interplanetary dust and other smaller objects. This family is called the Solar System, from *sol,* the Latin word for sun. The Sun is a star so enormous that over a million Earths could fit inside it! Because of its size, the Sun holds its nine planets in orbit around it. They are like weights, at the ends of invisible pieces of string,

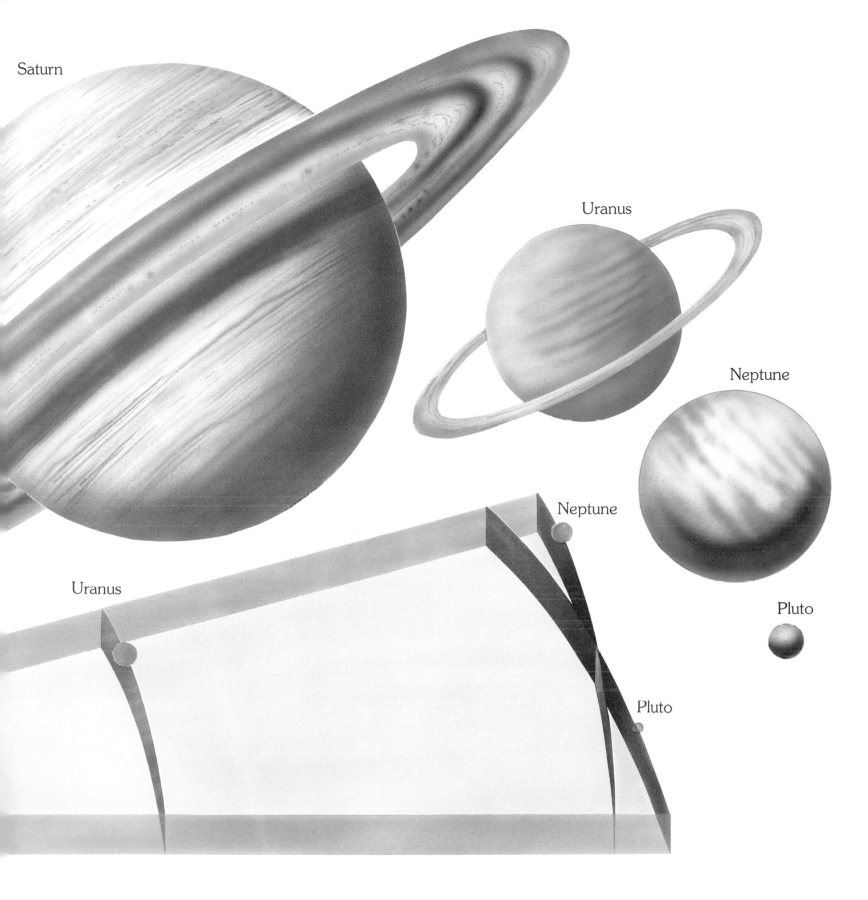

Saturn

Uranus

Neptune

Neptune

Uranus

Pluto

Pluto

being whirled around the sun, just as we might whirl a belt around our head. The force that keeps all these objects going round the Sun is called gravity. The closest planet to the Sun is Mercury, then Venus. Earth is the third from the Sun, and further out are Mars, Jupiter, Saturn, Uranus, and Neptune. Furthest out of all is Pluto, which is 80 times as far away from its neighbour, Neptune, as we are from the Sun. As the planets go round the Sun, so round some of the planets there are satellites revolving. The Moon is the Earth's satellite.

WHAT IS COAL?

Coal is a black or brown rock which can be found in layers, or seams, under the surface of the earth. It is made from the remains of giant ferns and trees that grew millions of years ago. When all this vegetation died, it rotted to become something called peat. As layer upon layer of peat was piled up, the bottom layers became cemented together as coal. Coal is one of the world's most important fuels.

HOW DO WE MEASURE TIME?

The basic unit for measurement is the day, the length of time that it takes for the Earth to go round once on its axis. A day is 24 hours, and in a year, which is the time taken for the Earth to go once round the Sun, there are about 365¼ days of 24 hours each. Because of that odd quarter-day, we have to have, every 4 years, a year with an extra full day in it: a Leap Year. A year is also divided into 12 months, and the months into weeks of 7 days. Hours are split into 60 minutes, and each minute into 60 seconds.

WHAT IS THE DIFFERENCE BETWEEN A HORSE AND A PONY?

The main difference is one of size. The height of both is measured in 'hands', with a hand being 10cm. The animal is always measured in a straight line from the ground to its withers, the ridge between its shoulder-bones. If the animal is 14.2 hands high or less, it is called a pony: over that height, it is a horse. Ponies usually have neat heads and small ears. Their ancestors lived in the wild, and were independent, so ponies are quicker-witted. Man has taken care of horses for centuries.

WHERE IS THE HIGHEST WATERFALL?

Neither of the world's most famous waterfalls are anywhere near the top ten as far as height is concerned. Niagara Falls, in the USA and Canada, is only 55 metres high, and Victoria Falls, between Zambia and Zimbabwe in Africa, is about 100 metres high. Four of the world's tallest falls are in South America. The biggest of all is Angel Falls in Venezuela, where the water drops over 800 metres. It is named after an American flier who crashed nearby in 1937.

Contents

First published 1993 by Brown Watson Ltd.
The Old Mill, 76 Fleckney Road.
Kibworth Beauchamp, Leicestershire. England
© 1993 Brown Watson Ltd.

ISBN 0 7097 0790-8

Printed in Belgium.